Which CUTE CREATURE Are You?

First published in Great Britain in 2026 by
Welbeck Children's Books
An imprint of Hachette Children's Group

Copyright © 2025 Hodder & Stoughton Limited

All rights reserved. This book is sold subject to the condition that it may not be reproduced, stored in a retrieval system, or transmitted in any form or by any means, electronic, mechanical, photocopying, recording, or otherwise, without the publisher's prior consent.

Welbeck Children's Books
An imprint of Hachette Children's Group
Part of Hodder & Stoughton Limited
Carmelite House
50 Victoria Embankment
London EC4Y 0DZ

An Hachette UK Company
www.hachette.co.uk
www.hachettechildrens.co.uk

The authorised representative in the EEA is Hachette Ireland, 8 Castlecourt Centre, Dublin 15, D15 XTP3, Ireland (email: info@hbgi.ie)

MIX
Paper | Supporting responsible forestry
FSC® C104740

ISBN: 978 1 80453 949 1
10 9 8 7 6 5 4 3 2 1
Printed in China

Which CUTE CREATURE Are You?

Written by
Grace Rockley

Illustrated by
Valeria Danilova

WELBECK
CHILDREN'S BOOKS

Answer the questions on each page to find out which cute creature you're most like ... it might surprise you!

Then read the fun facts to learn more about our furry (and not so furry) friends.

Are YOU an AXOLOTL?

Do you look HAPPY all of the time?

Do you prefer your own company rather than being out and about in a large group?

If YES, then you are an AXOLOTL!

DID YOU KNOW?

★ Axolotls have mouths that naturally go up at the corners, making them seem super-smiley.

★ Axolotls prefer being alone, but when they do want to find a mate they perform a dance by shaking their tail.

Are YOU a PYGMY HIPPO?

Do you feel more AWAKE at night than during the day?

Are you surprisingly fast?

If YES, then you are a PYGMY HIPPO!

DID YOU KNOW?

★ You won't find these hippos up and about during the day. Instead, they are active during the night when they can stroll along the river in peace.

★ Even though these cute hippos are small with short legs, they can run over 18 miles per hour. That's faster than the Olympic 800-metre champion!

Are YOU a RED PANDA?

Can your friends always spot you in a crowd?

Do you have LOTS of different nicknames?

If YES, then you are a RED PANDA!

The original panda!

Hey, Firefox!

Red-cat-bear?

No, that's a Himalayan raccoon!

You're a fox bear!

DID YOU KNOW?

 The white markings on red pandas' faces don't just make them extra cute, they also help their parents spot them in the dark.

 Red pandas are called all sorts of things. Some people call them 'firefox', 'red-cat-bear' or even 'lesser panda'. Rude!

Are YOU a DUCKLING?

QUACK QUACK!

TWEET TWEET!

Do you always have something to say? Do you LOVE chitchat?

Do you like to cuddle up when you're cold?

If YES, then you are a **DUCKLING!**

DID YOU KNOW?

 Ducklings love to chat. They start talking to each other before they've even hatched!

 Ducklings love to spend time with each other, especially when they're cold, so they can huddle together for warmth.

Are YOU a FENNEC FOX?

Are you an AMAZING listener?

Do you always want to win or be the BEST?

If YES, then you are a FENNEC FOX!

DID YOU KNOW?

 Fennec foxes' ears are around six inches long, which is HUGE for their small bodies. These help them listen out for any tasty treats moving underground and keep them cool. Phew!

 Fennec foxes are very competitive with each other when it is time to find a mate. They can be angry and fierce, so watch out ...

Are YOU a QUOKKA?

Do you wake up in some CRAZY positions after a cosy sleep?

Do you love to strike a pose and say 'cheese' for the camera?

If YES, then you are a QUOKKA!

DID YOU KNOW?

★ Quokkas often sleep in some funky positions. They like to curl up with their heads against their paws and tail, as if they are about to roll away ...

★ Many people take pictures with these quirky creatures while they flash their signature smile at the camera. These are called 'Quokka Selfies'!

Are YOU a SAND CAT?

Are you great at digging and building dens?

Do you hate to share?

If YES, then you are a SAND CAT!

DID YOU KNOW?

★ These wild desert cats dig into the ground to build underground homes called burrows. This gives them a great place to catch some z's and avoid the daytime sun.

★ They are animals that prefer to have a home all to themselves. If they have to share a burrow, they'll make sure to never be in it at the same time.

Are YOU a POMERANIAN?

Do you have long, shiny hair that needs LOTS of brushing?

Do you like to WOW a crowd with your party tricks?

If YES, then you are a POMERANIAN!

DID YOU KNOW?

 Pomeranians are known for having gorgeous fur, but that means these fuzzy friends need lots of trips to the groomer.

 They are the opposite of shy and often love to perform tricks to as many people as possible!

Are YOU a GIANT PANDA?

Do you have a favourite food that you could eat ALL day long?

Do you love gymnastics? Can you be found spinning round and upside down?

If YES, then you are a GIANT PANDA!

DID YOU KNOW?

★ Giant pandas will sometimes eat fish or other small animals, but they eat bamboo about 99 per cent of the time. That's a lot of bamboo!

★ Sometimes giant pandas do handstands up against a tree. This can be to relax or to mark their territory by leaving their scent.

Are YOU a SEA OTTER?

Do you like company as you fall asleep?

Do you have a favourite toy you take everywhere?

If YES, then you are a SEA OTTER!

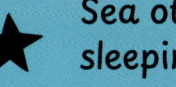

DID YOU KNOW?

 Sea otters often hold hands while they are sleeping. This is so the tide doesn't drift them apart as they drift off to sleep.

 They usually have a favourite rock that they carry around in a little pocket under their armpit. Sometimes they'll present it to someone special.

Extra FUN Facts

Axolotls don't have strong teeth, so they have to suck up their food. Luckily their favourite snacks are pretty slimy ...

For up to 17 hours a day, you'll find **red pandas** snoozing away. They LOVE to nap.

Fennec foxes have hairy feet to protect them from the hot sand. Do you take your fluffy slippers to the beach?

A **sea otter** can go its whole life without leaving the ocean.

Ducklings are born ready to get a move on. As soon as they hatch, they can walk, run and even jump.

Giant pandas are known to be shy and prefer the quiet life away from people.

Quokkas are great climbers and can get as high as five feet up a tree just to reach a tasty treat.

A **sand cat's** tail is about half of its body length. Sometimes sand cats bark like dogs. Woof!

Pomeranians often think they are bigger than they really are! This can lead to tricky times at the dog park ...

Pygmy hippos are one tenth the size of standard hippos. Do you think they're ten times as cute?

ENDANGERED Animals

WHAT DOES ENDANGERED MEAN?

An endangered animal is at risk of not existing anymore. This is called becoming extinct. Dinosaurs are an example of an animal that became extinct.

Some examples of endangered animals are red pandas, axolotls and sea otters.

HOW DO ANIMALS BECOME ENDANGERED?

There are lots of things that can lead to animals becoming endangered. Some of these are:

- Animals losing their homes from natural disasters or humans
- A change in climate meaning the animal, or their food, can no longer survive
- Humans taking the animals away

WHAT CAN WE DO?

It is important not to lose hope! Lots of animals that were endangered at one point aren't anymore, like the giant panda, which is no longer an endangered species. Here are some ways to help:

- Helping to protect the environment by not littering and reducing your carbon footprint
- Supporting places that help endangered animals, like wildlife reserves
- Telling your friends about endangered animals so they can help too

Cute Creature QUIZ

Time to put all the new things you have learnt to the test! Answer the questions without peeking. Then flip the page upside down to find out the answers.

1
What do axolotls shake when they want to find a mate?
a) their arms
b) their legs
c) their tails

2
How much bigger are standard hippos than pygmy hippos?
a) 10 times bigger
b) 20 times bigger
c) 50 times bigger

3
Which one of these is a common nickname for the red panda?
a) Ginger
b) Firefox
c) McFluffy

4
Fennec foxes' ears are around ...
a) 20 inches
b) 2 inches
c) 6 inches

5
What do ducklings do to warm themselves up?

a) huddle up
b) swim extra fast
c) quack louder

6
Sand cats can make a sound like which animal?

a) a dog
b) a duck
c) a lion

7
Pomeranians often think they are _____ than they really are. Which word fills in the blank?

a) louder
b) bigger
c) more flexible

8
Quokkas are known for...

a) singing
b) taking great selfies
c) fighting

9
Roughly how much of a giant panda's diet is bamboo?

a) 100%
b) 99%
c) 80%

10
Sea otters sometimes carry rocks in a little pocket under their...

a) tummy
b) ear
c) armpit

Answers
1. c, 2. a, 3. b, 4. c, 5. a, 6. a, 7. b, 8. b, 9. b, 10. c